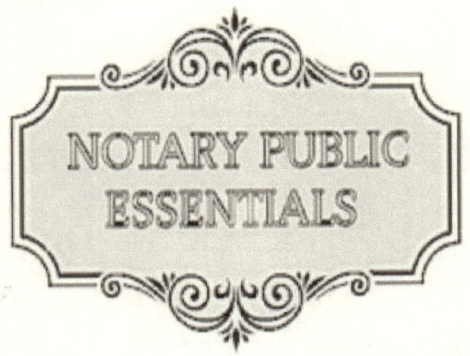

Helpful knowledge for all Commissioned Notaries
in the United States of America

Remote Notary-eNotary-Mobile Notary-Traditional Notary

Jeannie Eunice Franks

Notary Public and Certified Notary Signing Agent

Notary Public Essentials

Self Published by Jeannie Eunice Franks
Commonwealth of Virginia
United States of America

Notary Public Essentials
ISBN 978-1-387-88753-8

Visit: https://www.VirginiaNotary.club
https://www.facebook.com/MyVirginiaNotary

Join my Network of Professionals:
https://www.linkedin.com/in/jeannie-franks-490453167/

OATH

I, _____, having been duly appointed and commissioned a Notary Public in and for the Commonwealth of _____, do solemnly swear (or affirm) that I will support, obey and defend the Constitution of the United States and the Constitution of this State and that I will discharge the duties of my office with fidelity.

Dedicated to:

My parents who always taught me to do the right thing,

my husband who supports me in everything I do,
my colleagues who also pursue greatness for our Nation,
to the people of the Unites Sates of America,
to the United States of America; the land of the free and the home of the brave,
to the people who I constantly learn from,
to the people behind the designs and development of the
accessories/resources Notaries need when providing services,
and to the insurance companies that protect the public and Notaries.

May the content of this book be easy to understand. However, I encourage you to pursue further readings published by your state and other commissioned Notaries.

This book starts with Remote and Electronic Notarization because, as Technology becomes more embedded in our everyday lives, notarial acts are also catching up with the system transforming the way Notarial Acts are provided.

Do your best, and as you become a great Notary Public, share your story, tips you have learned, and the good habits you have acquired so, when new Notaries enter the field, they can also contribute to the safety and prosperity of the United States of America.

Jeannie Eunice Franks-Belgrave

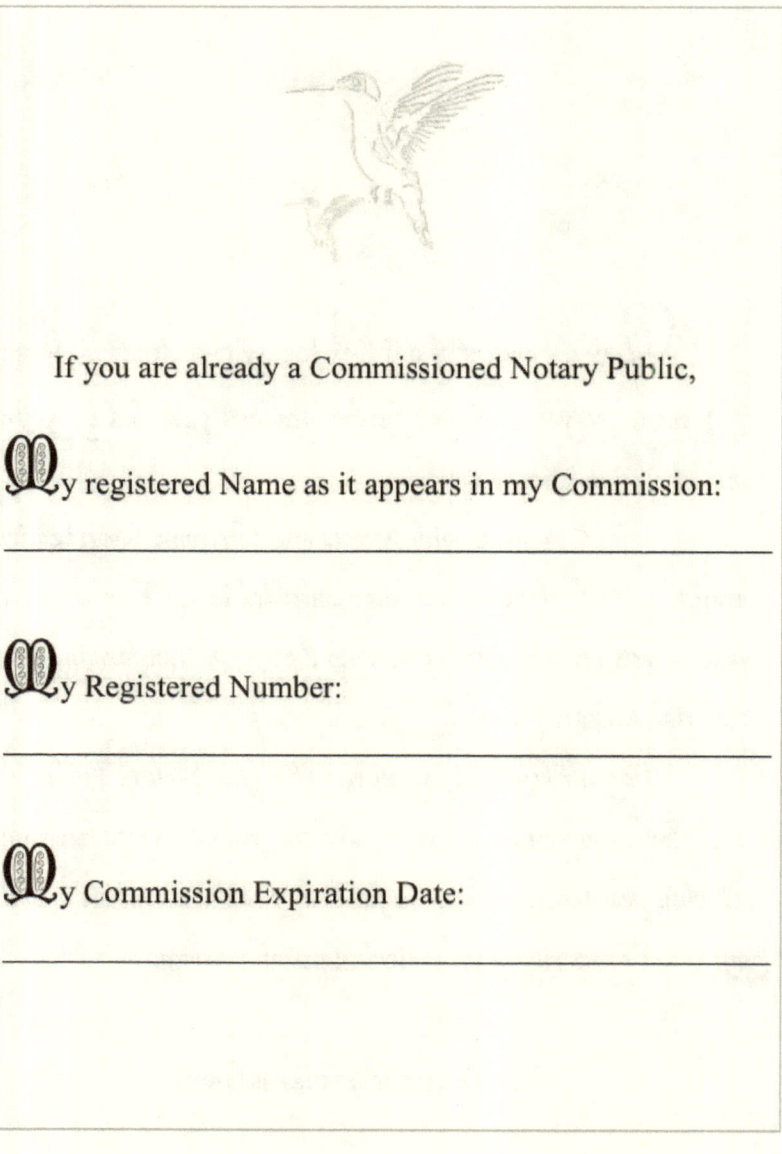

If you are already a Commissioned Notary Public,

My registered Name as it appears in my Commission:

_____

My Registered Number:

_____

My Commission Expiration Date:

_____

Contents

Other works by the Author:

Remote/WebCam Notarization
Basic Understanding

Prologue: 𝒯he recording of important documents and signatures have been part of human history for centuries. The purpose of this book is to bring to you, the reader, practical understanding of essential elements found within the notarial field in the United States of America. Having people from all over the world living in the USA, it is important to know that notarial acts in United States vary when compared to notarial acts in other countries. For example, in Latin America, notaries have some of the powers a licensed lawyer has in the United States while in United States, non-lawyers notaries cannot provide legal advice. Also, it is essential to have in mind that each State and Commonwealth within the United States of America has its own laws. If you are reading this book because you want to become a Notary Public or already have a commission, remember to always review the Notary Handbook of the State or Commonwealth that commissioned you.

The content of this book also intends to provide notary public essentials that will be helpful to remote notaries, eNotaries, mobile notaries, and traditional notaries. Whoever you decide to be or are apply **Reasonable Care** which, according to the NNA, *it is generally defined in law as the degree of attentiveness and precaution that would be exercised by a person of ordinary prudence and intelligence. (5 Steps To A Flawless Notarization,* page 5).

Brief History: Notary Public is one of the oldest professions in existence. It dates back to ancient Egypt followed by ancient Roman Times when few people were taught to read and write. Notaries are the oldest continuing branch of the legal profession. In ancient history, those who adopted a method coined as shorthand were termed *notarius or scribes* and were responsible for recording shorthand statements and later transcriptions of such materials into formal memoranda.

In Europe, notary public remained a figured of importance and was maintained throughout the *Dark Ages* and *Italian Renaissance* as a central institution of law.

United Kingdom had its first notaries during the late fourteenth century appointed by the *Papal Legate* and were often members of the clergy. In 1533, after the abolition of the *Papal Legate*, the King had the authority to appoint notary positions.

In United States of America, the rendering of notarial acts could be traced back to *Colonial Times* when only persons of high moral character were appointed as Notaries to certify and keep documents safe.

Current Role of a Notary Public in USA

Now-a-days, unlike most countries, a great percentage of people commissioned as a notary public in the United States are not licensed attorneys-at-law admitted to the bar. Generally speaking, a U.S. notary public is a person appointed by a state government to serve the public as an impartial witness. The notary is considered a State officer, whether the jurisdiction is Common law or Civil law. As of today, Louisiana is the only civil law state within the United States. Now, lets see what is the difference between Common Law and Civil Law.

Main differences between Common Law and Civil Law

The American legal system is based on English Common Law with the exception of Louisiana which is based on Civil Law. Surprised? Yes, United States of America's law system is greatly influenced by the English System.

Common Law is uncodified; no comprehensive compilation of legal rules and statutes while the Civil Law is codified; comprehensive, continuously updated legal codes that specify all matters capable of being brought before a court, the applicable procedure, and the appropriate punishment for each offense. As Notary Public, you do not need to worry about this. Just check the rules of your state and abide by them.

Now, if you happen to be a lawyer to licensed within the jurisdiction of United States of America, please, ask your mentor in law how to best practice your duties as a Notary Public.

|

Remember: IN UNITED STATES OF AMERICA, IF YOU ARE NOT A LAWYER, THEN, **AS A NOTARY PUBLIC, YOU CANNOT OFFER OR PROVIDE LEGAL ADVICE.**

In the Commonwealth of Virginia, for example, there is a Code that reads:
Section 47.1-15.1. of the Code of Virginia, a *notary public shall not offer or provide legal advice.*

Always check the laws of the State you are commissioned at.

Your role as a **Notary Public** is explained by the job description in itself: as defined by 123Notary.com, a Notary Public is *an official authorized by law to act as an **impartial witness** to signatures, administer oaths, authenticate copies of documents, attest to signatures made by individuals, and perform other notary acts permitted within his or her jurisdiction.* If you noticed, I bolded "Impartial witness." This is a concept that every notary public needs to embed in his or her notarial acts.

Impartial = unbiased.

Also, another important aspect of Notaries is the ability to deter fraud. In a way, when a person is commissioned as a public officer to provide Notary Service, there is also an obligation to deter fraudulent attempts. This is another way to keep our communities safe and free from illicit attempts that are linked to the signing of important documents.

As mentioned by the American Society of Notaries:
Notaries are expected to know and honor what their state laws allow them to do.

Electronic Notary (eNotary) and Remote Notary

Electronic Notary (eNotary) vs WebCam or Remote Notary:

/\   /\

In-person presence of client **required**   In-Person presence of client **not required**

It is important that Commissioned Electronic Notaries are familiar with The Uniform Electronic Transactions Act (UETA) completed by the Uniform Law Commissioners of the National Conference of Commissioners on Uniform State Law in 1999. According to the American Society of Notaries, *UETA removed barriers to electronic commerce by establishing equal legal status between electronic transactions and signatures and those that involve paper.*

By now, you may have heard of eNotary or Electronic Notary services. If you have not yet, there is a great possibility that the State you live in has not approved electronic notary services yet. Electronic notarization is expanding and transforming the way documents are notarized. eNotaries seem to be more in demand as the service is known. For example, I remember the first time I found out about the eNotarization services. Back then, I was a Traditional Commissioned Notary Public at a state that did not allow electronic notarizations. I needed a document notarized and sent to an office located in the Commonwealth of Virginia, my soon to be home. An eNotary from Virginia offered me the service which was also considered a Remote Notary Service. From Oklahoma, I was able to get a document notarized in Virginia thanks to the electronic notarization with WebCam or Remote Notarization technology allowed in the Commonwealth of Virginia.

How does anyone become an electronic Notary or eNotary?

First, the person needs to be Commissioned as a traditional Notary Public, at least this is how it is in the Commonwealth of Virginia, and I do not see why it would be different in the other states and Commonwealths where electronic notarization has been approved.

Be prepared to invest in State fees, seals, forms (both paper and self-inked stamps), Record books, the hardware needed for electronic notarization and marketing.

Benefits of electronic Notarizations:

-Less paper printed*
-Less ink used*
-Secured through encrypted technology.
-Convenience.

*I recommend to always keep a hardcopy of notarial acts. Even though a digital logbook might be enough, there is no harm in printing out the digital book and safeguarding it the way the traditional Notarial acts are safeguarded.

Benefits of Remote Notarization

-Client saves in miles fees charged by mobile notaries.
-Remote Notarization can be done from the comfort
of home or office using Audiovisual equipment such
as a WebCam.

There are many companies and individuals that need documents notarized fast. Electronic Notarization and the use of audiovisual equipment provide the convenience, safety, and security needed 24/7 as long as the internet operates proficiently and the hardware and software used by the eNotary and the hardware and software used by the other end users are well maintained.

What can be Notarized electronically?

It depends on the state. Remember, all states may belong to the same country, but each state in the United States of America has its own laws.

For example, in the Commonwealth of Virginia, the following electronic notarial acts are allowed:

- Take acknowledgments;
- Administer oaths and affirmations (e.g., Jurats);
- Certify affidavits or depositions;
- Certify "true copies" of documents;
- Perform a verification of fact.

Check your state to see what notarial acts are allowed and if they need to be electronically recorded and stored.

Remote Notarizations

Here is when a signer personally appears before the Notary at the time of the **notarization using audio-visual technology** over the internet instead of being physically present in the same room. Webcam notarization is also called remote notarization or online notarization.

Remote Notarization vs Electronic Notarization

Webcam notarization (Remote) makes use of video and audio technology on the internet to allow signers to personally appear and communicate with the Notary at the time of the notarization.

Electronic or e-Notary is essentially the same as traditional "paper" notarization except that the document is being notarized in digital form and the Notary signs with an electronic signature.

As technology picks up and people catch up with technology, I believe electronic and remote notarizations will be more common in the United States of America.

Online companies used by Notaries today

Here are the most popular:

In order to obtain a secured personalized Digital Certificate, I recommend *IdenTrust*.

To sign documents online, here are popular apps:

Notarize
DocVerify
Notarycam
Safedocs
SIGNix

I also recommend having **Adobe** products installed in your computer.

Essential Vocabulary eNotaries and Remote Notaries need to be familiar with:

Digital Certificate:
This is your secured information used over the internet using a public key infrastructure.

Public Key Infrastructure (PKI):
Is a Certificate of Authority (CA) which issue digital certificates that authenticate the identity of organizations and individuals over a public system such as the internet.

Certificate of Authority (CA):
Is a trusted entity that issues electronic documents that verify a digital entity's identity on the internet.

Digital Signature:
a type of electronic signature that encrypts documents with digital codes that are particularly difficult to duplicate. Digital Signature is not the same as Digital Certificate.

Portable Document Format (PDF):
a file format that provides an electronic image of text or text and graphics that looks like a printed document and can be viewed, printed, and electronically transmitted.

Smart card:
a plastic card with a built-in microprocessor, used typically for electronic processes such as financial transactions and personal identification.

Card Reader:
is the generic term for an input device that reads flash memory cards. It can be a standalone device that connects to a computer via USB or it may be integrated into a computer, printer, or multifunction device. As the name suggests, its purpose is to read the inserted card.

USB token:
is a physical device that is used to establish personal identity without use of a password to access a network. A USB token is used to prove the user's identity electronically, thus enhancing digital security. It provides secure and strong authentication for network access.

WebCam with audio capability:
a video camera that inputs to a computer connected to the Internet, so that its images can be viewed by Internet users.

Do you still want to become an eNotary and Remote Notary?

-Review your state laws for eNotaries and Remote.
-Be ready to invest money and time.
-Apply to become a Traditional Notary.
-Study the Notary Handbook provided by the State or Commonwealth you are applying at.
-Take good care of your health. Notaries need a sharp mind and organizational skills.
- After applying, be patient. It might take a couple of weeks or more to get an answer from your local government.
- Maintain your electronic equipment updated, free of viruses, and defragmented so it always runs smoothly when performing remote and electronic notarial acts.

REMEMBER:

eNotarization and Remote Notarizations are transforming the way notarial acts are done. Always review your State or Commonwealth laws for Notaries.

Here is a link eNotaries should check from time to time:

http://www.npa-section.com/electronic-notarization.html

Traditional Notary Public Essential

𝒜 Notary Public is a public officer and an impartial witness when providing notarial services.

Although eNotaries seem to be more in demand now-a-days, notaries, in general, need to learn from the basic traditional notarial concepts and protocol. In other words, an eNotary cannot be an eNotary without the founding training received as traditional Notary Public.

What are the steps to become a Traditional Notary Public?

-Review the current laws that pertain to Notarial acts in the state or Commonwealth where the Notary Public application will be submitted.

-Be prepared to invest time and money. Everything the Notary Public will need will cost something. Example: application fees, seals, stamps, Log book, Lock bag, paper forms, self-inked stamps, marketing material, Notary Public courses if needed, and so on.

- Fill out the Application Form and pay the application fee.

-Be patient while the local Government reviews the application.

- After receiving the Commission, order seals, stamps, and all the necessary accessories for notarial acts.

-Join a Notary Public Association. Usually, through the association, Notaries get discounts, updated information, and more.

- Depending on the state, a bond might be needed. Read the State Laws to find out.

- Regardless of the state or Commonwealth, buy an Errors & Omission Insurance (E & O Insurance) for the amount of years the Notary Public Commission is active; usually four years.

-Keep your integrity and great organizational skills.

-Enjoy when handling paperwork.

-Have great attention to detail.

-Provide great Customer Service.

-Study the Notary Handbook or Manual of your state or Commonwealth so your natural ability to explain concepts increases.

-Take great care of your health. Notaries need a sharp mind not only to render Notarial Services effectively but also to deter fraud and recognize coercion.

Mobile Notary Public Essentials

$\mathcal{A}$ mobile notary could be a Traditional Notary and an Electronic Notary. The Remote Notary, if he or she has to drive somewhere to get the remote notarization done, he or she can also be considered mobile notary. However, it is more common to understand it as the notary who is willing to drive to the client's place or the place agreed by both the client and the notary. The idea is that the mobile notary makes it more convenient to the client to get documents notarized.

Essentially, a Mobile Notary is a commissioned Notary Public who drives somewhere to get the notarial act done. Many Mobile Notaries are available 24/7 including holidays.

Being a Mobile Notary has advantages such as providing notary services to people who cannot go to you, the Notary.

As Mobile Notary, always have your vehicle well maintained and with enough gas. Also, have your Notary Tools inside a locked Notary bag.

Have your Notary ID on you, and always be presentable and polite no matter how bad was the traffic or weather.

What are the most common types of Notarial Acts? In my experience, they are:

Acknowledgements:

The main purpose of this notarial act is to ensure that the signer of the document is who he or she claim to be. Acknowledgments are often needed for documents concerning valuable assets such as deeds, mortgages, and deeds of trusts.
The Acknowledgment must be a part of the original document.
This can be done by placing the acknowledgment language in the document itself or by adding the language in a separate paper that is attached to the original.

Jurats:

This is where the signer swears or affirm that the content of the document is true. A Jurat is the clause added at the foot of an affidavit.

What is an Affidavit? Is a written statement under oath or affirmation.

Oaths/Affirmations:

Oath is a Solemn pledge to a Supreme Being.
Affirmation is a solemn pledge to the individual's honor.

Copy Certification:

In order to render notarial act, client provides ORIGINAL document (s). Make sure to check the laws of the State or Commonwealth.
For example: in the Commonwealth of Virginia, notaries cannot certify copies of Birth Certificates, Marriage Certificates, and Death Certificates.

Signature Witnessing:

This is when the notary just need to witness the signing of a document without having to administer an Oath or an Affirmation.

IDENTIFYING THE SIGNER (S)
I recommend the following but always review your State or Commonwealth's laws.

The presented ID must be valid and have, at least the following: Name, age, description of the signer, issue date, who issued it, and expiration date. Also the ID must have, at least, the same information as the document. Asking for a current driver's license helps because it will present a current picture of the signer. If the signer does not have a current driver's license because the person does not drive, sometimes States issue non-driver IDs. Keep asking for current documentation that have a current picture of the signer.

At some point, you may be faced with a signer that will place an "X" as a signature. In this case, the signer will need "credible witnesses" that will confirm and sign the form as well and sign the Notary's LogBook.
What is a credible witness? Someone who knows the signer, who is willing to swear or affirm that the person who is signing is who he or she claims to be, and is willing to sign your Notary Journal possibly adding his or her thumb print as well.

Although some States do not require to keep a LogBook, do your best to always record details of notarial acts in your Notary's LogBook. As far as I know, it is not against the law to keep a Notary LogBook even is the State or Commonwealth does not require it. Always ask your Secretary of State though specially if you, as Notary, are planning to record thumb prints on your LogBook.

How many credible witness do you need? Each state and Commonwealth seems to have its own rule on it. Verify the amount of Credible Witness needed with your State or Commonwealth.

Why will a person sign with an "X"?
This is known as "Signature by mark". The most known reasons have to do with medical issues or disabilities.

Do your best to make sure that the person who is in front of you either in person or remotely is the person who he or she says he or she is. This is a Notary's first line of responsibility followed by a good implementation of # notarial tools.

The more you are in the front line of notarization, the more you will realize that there are many people who will try to trick you. Remember, if you the Notary have a reason to reject a notarization, do it. If something does not seem right or you feel that intuitive field in you telling you don't do it, follow it. In my life, I've learned that intuition is usually right. The more educated you are in the Notary Field, your intuition will be right there with you alerting you of invisible red flags. Your eyes and your education will alert you of the visible red flags flashing during a notarization process.

There are States that allow the Notary to vouch for the signer if the Notary personally knows the signer. Check your State's Notary laws for it.

ORGANIZATIONS

In my experience as Notary, being part of an organization that supports Notaries has been helpful. Here are a few recommended ones:

American Association of Notaries
https://secure.usnotaries.net

National Notary Association
https://www.nationalnotary.org.

American Society of Notaries
https://www.asnnotary.org/

Notary Rotary
https://www.notaryrotary.com/

Lousiana Notary Association
https://lna.org/

Pennsylvania Association of Notaries
https://www.notary.org/

Florida Mobile Notary Association, Inc.
http://www.flmna.org/

ONLINE FORUMS & FACEBOOK PAGES

Staying on top of the game means having access and a presence online. Get a dedicated website for your Notary Public services, Facebook page, Instagram, Youtube, Google+, etc. Have a constant presence and image. What do I mean by that? Get a logo that will represent your presence when you visit forums and promote your services online.

To get a logo at a very good price and excellent customer service, visit:

https://jeanniefranks1.wixsite.com/dlogosnow

https://www.facebook.com/dLogosNow

Forums and other Facebook pages

http://www.123notary.com/

https://notarycafe.com

https://www.facebook.com/groups/
notary.signing.agent.network/

https://www.facebook.com/groups/260894657592038/

https://www.facebook.com/groups/
ProfessionalNotaryNetwork/

Essential Vocabulary
among Notaries

Acknowledgment: A formal declaration made to authoritative witness by the person who executed the document that it was freely executed.

Acknowledgment Certificate: A written statement, affixed to an agreement, signed and sealed by an authorized official that states in a form, usually prescribed by law, that the official took the acknowledgment of the person who signed the agreement.

Administer: To give or apply in a formal way.

Affiant: One who makes a swearing statement in an affidavit.

Affidavit: A written declaration made under oath before a notary public or other authorized officer.

Affirmation: To declare positively or firmly; maintain to be true.

Apostille: Authentication document or endorsement instituted by The Hague Convention and many times required as additional authentication for international acceptance.

Attest: To affirm to be correct, true, or genuine; corroborate.

Authenticate: To prove or verify as genuine.

Certified Copy: A document certified by a notary to be a true and correct copy of the original.

Civil Liability: The responsibility and obligation to make compensation to another person for damages caused by improper performance of duties and acts.

Commission: A document describing the notary's appointment and term of office.

Credible Witness: A believable witness worthy of confidence. Creates a chain of personally known individuals from the notary public to the signer of a document.

Embosser: A pliers-like device, that when squeezed together with paper between the jaws, makes raised areas and indentations on paper. Used as a protection device. Not an official notary seal; but may be used in addition to the official notary seal. Some States may require it. Check the laws of the State or Commonwealth.

Errors and Omission Insurance: a professional insurance policy designed for the protection of the notary when held liable for honest mistakes. The insurance often covers both court costs and settlement.

Impartial Witness: unbiased without personal interest in the process.

Jurat: An affidavit declaring when, where, and before whom it was sworn.

Jurisdiction/Venue: The locality where a cause of action occurs. The state and county where a notarization takes place.

Loose Certificate: A document with notarial wording that is separate from, and attached to, the document being notarized. It is used when no wording is provided on the document, when that provided wording does not comply with the state's requirements, when there is no room for the notary seal on the document, or when a pre-printed certificate has already been used by another notary in the case of multiple signers.

Notary Journal: An official record book of notarizations performed by a notary. Required by law in several states. All entries must be in chronological order and have all required fields completed at the time of notarization. If must be kept under the direct and exclusive control of the notary and kept in locked and/or secured area.

Notary Public: A person commissioned by a state government or Commonwealth to serve the public as an impartial witness with duties specified by law. The notary has the power to witness the signing of documents and to administer oaths.

Notary Seal: An official stamp or embosser used by a notary to seal notarizations. Safeguard your seals.

Notary Signing Agent: Trained and certified Notary specialized in obtaining and notarizing the signatures of the party (ies) involved on real state loan documents.

Oath: A statement by a person who asserts it to be true, calling upon a Higher Being as witness.

Personally Known: Familiarity with an individual resulting from interactions with that individual over a period of time sufficient to eliminate every reasonable doubt that the individual has the identity claimed.

Power of Attorney: A legal instrument authorizing one to act as another's agent or attorney.

Rescind: to cancel.

Subscribe: To sign one's name in attestation, testimony, or consent.

Subscribing Witness: A person who appears before the notary on behalf of the principal. The subscribing witness must have been requested and/or authorized by the principal to get the document notarized, must swear under oath or affirmation that they either saw the principal sign the document or heard the principal acknowledge that they signed the document, must sign the document before appearing in from of the notary or in the notary's presence, must establish identity through personal knowledge of the notary or through the oath or affirmation of a credible witness known to the subscribing witness and the notary, and must sign the notary's journal.

Suspend: To cause to stop for a period; interrupt.

Swear/Sworn: To make a solemn promise; to vow, usually before a Higher Being.

Testimonium clause: At the end of many documents and certificates that follows the form "witness my hand and seal" or some variation thereof.

Venue / Jurisdiction: The locality where a cause of action occurs. The state and county where a notarization takes place.

Verification: A confirmation of the truth of a theory or fact.

Witness: A person who watches an action take place.

Developing Good Habits

1) **D**evelop good notary public habits from the moment you decide and **commit** to become a Notary Public. The foundation of your Notary Public service begins with you, the Notary Public. You are in charge of your character, how you present yourself to others, and how you view yourself as a Notary Public.

2) **F**rom conversations I have had with other notaries and even my own experience as a Notary Public, anxiety may be triggered at the beginning of your Notary Public service. That is a normal feeling. One may study and learn rules, but when it comes to having people and their paperwork in front of you, emotions may come into play. The more Notarial Acts you perform, the easier it gets because your eyes become naturally accustomed to documents, and your hands become used to taking the pre-inked seal, embosser, the log-book, etc. Also, some people are born with the ability to interact with other people, if you find yourself being quite not that extroverted, it is acceptable too. The most important part of a Notarial Act is that you know what to do and what not to do.

3) Another important good habit is to keep your Notary Seals, Logbook or Notary Public Journal, Digital Certificate, passwords, and everything related to your Notary Service in one place and most likely locked. Be preventive, safeguard your tools and the information you obtain from the clients who trusted you the moment they requested your Notary Public Service.

4) If you are able to, be the only User on the computer or electronic devices that you utilize to perform Remote Notarial Acts or eNotary. Keep your files organized, secure them with passwords, and be the only one with administrator permission.

5) When providing remote notarization services, make sure you are in a private space where your internet connection is secured. Please, do not go to a public place that provides free-wifi and handle the notarization from there. Remember, you are dealing with private information.

6) When performing notarial acts in person, identify the signer first, then log the information in the Notary Public Journal, eye-scan* the document, and finally perform the notarial act. Making it a habit will give you, the Notary, more time to assess if the signer is who she or

he says she or he is, if the signer is not being coerced, and if the document has blank spaces or needs Notarial wording. Remember, as Notary Public, you have the right to refuse to notarize any document when you suspect that the signer's identification is questionable, the signer might not be there in her or his own will, or the signer does not know what type of notarial act she or he wants. The latter one is common when the document lacks of notarial wording. As Notary Public, you can explain the signer the different types of notarial acts, but cannot decide for the signer which one to apply to the document. By doing so, it could be taken as a legal advice. If the signer still does not know, the next best thing to do is to advise the signer to contact the agency where the document originated from so the agency can let the signer know which notarial act will be needed. This is why it is important to follow the steps in the order described at the beginning so it becomes a good natural habit.

*eye-scan: there are documents that contain very private information and, as Notary, you are only looking for completeness and notarial wording. Remember, as notary, you are notarizing a signature or certifying a copy (where allowed) not the content of the document.

7) Always take control of the notarial act. Many signers are oblivious of the responsibilities of a Notary and they might be tempted to rush the moment. Do not fall for it even if you know the person. Apply your rules, follow your order of steps. As Notary, you might not be making a

fortune, but you can make your notarial act right every time.

8) Network with other notaries who speak different languages beside English. Even though English is the primary language and the language Notarial Acts in the United States of America, there will be moments when clients will speak other languages, documents may come to you written in other languages or the signer might not be able to speak English at all. Have a backup. This way, even if you are not able to notarize the document due to language barriers, at least, you are able to provide customer service and/or direct the signer to someone who can help.

9) Take great care of your health. Make it a natural thing to you. Wake up early, eat healthy, keep your mind positive, laugh at least once every day. It will enhance your journey as a Notary Public.

10) Read Notary Public related information specially if it is information from your State or Commonwealth. One never knows when a new law may be added or another one amended. It is better to be informed.

11) Let everyone know you are a Notary Public.

12) $\mathbf{I}$ highly recommend that you get a Notary ID that identifies you as Notary Public. We ask for people's IDs, so, it will only be proper for them to see an ID on us that has our name as it is shown in the Notary Registration, our picture, commission number, expiration day, and the logo we identify with when promoting our services. Here is the link to a website I ordered mine from.

https://www.idcreator.com/badge-maker#mydesigns

13) $\mathbf{D}$O YOUR HOMEWORK. I can guide you through, but each situation is on its own. Do not wait until the last minute to get familiar with concepts or how I should do this or that. Read this book as many times as you need to until it becomes second nature to you. Read other Notarial Acts material until they become second nature to you. Make it a natural habit to pick up a book and read the vocabulary related to notarial acts.

14) $\mathbf{K}$eep your notarial tools clean and safe.

15) $\mathbf{C}$arry with you hand sanitizer. Before you grab your notarial tools, sanitize your hands. the last thing you want is to get sick. Always stay on top of your healthy habits. Keeping your hands clean is not exception.

16) Always be presentable even if you live one block from the beach and people go to your house for notarial acts. Always be presentable even if you have spent all your money in getting your Notary Commission, notarial tools, and marketing together. Remember, money does not make who you are or your character.

17) Be always polite no matter what. Once commissioned, you become a public officer or official. Always project good character and politeness.

18) In case I did not mention this before, keep your notarial tools together, clean, out of the reach of anybody else; children, adult, pets; among the notarial tools, keep a portable hard surface in case the clients you travel to for notarial acts do not have a clean flat surface available. I am thinking about keeping a portable mini table in my car. How about you?

Tips to Remember

A Notary Public is not authorized to give legal advice or to prepare legal documents on behalf of others.

If there is not enough room for you, the notary, to sign and place your seal in the notarization area on a document, affix a certificate.

If your notary commission has expired, you cannot continue to use your expired seal.

A Notary Bond is required in some states and it protects the public against a notary's misconduct or negligence.

An Errors & Omission Insurance (E & O Insurance) might not be required but it is highly recommended that each Notary Public gets one, preferably for the amount of years of the commission.

Documents are notarized with the purpose of ensuring that the signer or signers of a document are who they say they are and to deter fraud.

A Notary Public is an impartial witness. Impartial meaning that the Notary has no bias toward the document being notarized.

Notary fees are optional. If charged, fees should be according to the State or Commonwealth laws. Fees charged should be recorded for reporting tax purposes.

A notary may decline notarization if the signer is under the influence of drugs or alcohol, the signer is mentally incapable of making decisions, the signer does not provide acceptable identification, or if the notary suspects fraud.

The notary journal is the exclusive property of the notary public and is required to be secured under the exclusive control of the notary at all times.

When providing traditional notary services, identify the signer first by asking adequate identification. Eye-scan the document to be notarized. Open your notarial journal and input the required information. Make sure the client signs your journal as well. If possible, get the client's thumb print on your journal. Then, proceed to notarize the document.

If you decide to become an electronic and Remote Notary Public, take great care of your electronic equipment. Get familiar with the terms used in the digital environment you will be dealing with as eNotary or Remote Notary.

Essential Marketing Strategy

Once you have received your commission as Notary Public, get a logo that speaks to you, a logo or design that you identify with, that inspires you when you see it, a logo that you will gladly promote along with your Notary Services.

If you need assistance with your logo, check
https://jeanniefranks1.wixsite.com/dlogosnow
or
https://www.facebook.com/dLogosNow/

You can also Google #dLogosNow

To order your marketing material and get a discount the first time you order, go to:

http://reward.vistaprint.com/go.axd?ref=KFWVV1

(It is my hope that the link above will be active by the time you read this book).

Find out about local events where you can network.

Network, network, network. Let people know you are a Notary Public.

Always have your business card with your logo and most essential information on it.
Create a page on Facebook. Mine is:
https://www.facebook.com/MyVirginiaNotary/

Feel free to like it and contact me via Facebook.

Find out what places usually require notarization services. If you want more ideas, visit my website:
https://www.virginianotary.club/

Creativity is key in your journey as Notary Public.

If you speak Spanish and want Spanish clients to request your services, please, make sure you advertise your services to the Spanish speaking population as "Notary Public" and not *Notario Público*. Check your State or Commonwealth Handbook. Most likely you will find that advertising your services as *Notario Público* is not appropriate.

It is known that a Notary Public in countries located in LatinAmerica has other powers a Notary Public in the United States of America does not have.
At least, in the Commonwealth of Virginia it is illegal to promote Notary Public services using the words *Notario Público*.

|

Essential Books

Notary Public Essentials. Jeannie Eunice Franks. 2018

Electronic and Remote Notarizations. Jeannie Eunice Franks. 2018

Five Steps to Flawless Notarization. Published by NNA.

Current ID Checking Guide, U.S. & Canada Edition.

Current I.D. Checking Guide, International Edition.

There are other books sold by the organizations mentioned below.

American Association of Notaries
http://www.notarypublicstamps.com/notary-seals/
virginia/#Books

National Notary Association
https://www.nationalnotary.org/supplies/notary-books

Sample FORMS

Here are sample forms. Check your State or Commonwealth Notary Handbook. Also, when you order self inked stamps from a trust source, the source usually knows what goes in the self-inked stamp.

· ·

OATH

Notary Public's Oath of Office

State of _____) SS:

County of _____

I, _____, having been duly appointed and commissioned a Notary Public in and for the State of _____, do solemnly swear (or affirm) that I will support, obey and defend the Constitution of the United States and the Constitution of this State and that I will discharge the duties of my office with fidelity.

· ·

Commonwealth of _____) SS:

County of _____

I, _____, having been duly appointed and commissioned a Notary Public in and for the Commonwealth of _____, do solemnly swear (or affirm) that I will support, obey and defend the Constitution of the United States and the Constitution of this State and that I will discharge the duties of my office with fidelity.

AFFIDAVIT

An affidavit is a voluntary, sworn written statement.

The name of the affiant, the person giving the statement, must be mentioned in the affidavit and the affiant is required to sign the affidavit in the notary's presence.

An Affidavit would look something like this:

....

State of _____))SS:County of _____)

Before me, the undersigned notary public, this day, personally, appeared_____ to me known, who being duly sworn according to law, deposes the following:

(Affiant's Statement)

_____ (Signature of Affiant)

Subscribed and sworn to before me this_____day of_____, 20___.

_____ Notary Public

My Commission Expires: _____

Acknowledgment (State)

State of _____
County of _____
Before me, (insert the name and character of the
officer), on this day personally appeared
_____, known to me (or proved to me on
the oath of _____ or through (description of
identity card or other document) to be the person whose
name is subscribed to the foregoing instrument and
acknowledged to me that he executed the same for the
purposes and consideration therein expressed.
Given under my hand and seal of office this _____
day of _____, (year).

(Personalized Seal) Notary Public's Signature

Short Version of Acknowledgement (State)

State of _____
County of _____
This instrument was acknowledged before me on (date) by
(name or names of person or persons acknowledging).

(Seal)

_____
Notary Public's Signature

Notary Public Essentials

Acknowledgement (Commonwealth)

Commonwealth of _____
County of _____
The foregoing instrument was acknowledged before me this ___ day of _____, 20 ___,
by _____ (name of person acknowledged).

_____
Signature of Notarial Officer_____
Notary Registration Number: _____
My Commission Expires: _____

(Seal)

··

Acknowledgment for Corporation

Commonwealth of_____
County of _____
The foregoing instrument was acknowledged before me
_____this _____day by _____ (name of
officer or agent, title of officer or agent) of
_____(name of corporation acknowledging) a
_____ (state or place of incorporation)
corporation, on behalf of the corporation.

Seal

_____
(Signature of Person Taking Acknowledgment)
(Title or Rank) (Serial Number, if any)

Notary's Registration Number:_____

Acknowledgment for Attorney-in-fact

```
Commonwealth of_____
County of _____
The foregoing instrument was acknowledged before me
_____ this _____ (date) by _____
(name of attorney-in-fact), as attorney-in-fact on
behalf of _____ (name of principal).


 Seal             _____
 (Signature of Person Taking Acknowledgment)
 (Title or Rank) (Serial Number, if any)
  Notary's Registration Number:_____
```

....

Jurat

```
Commonwealth of _____
City/County of _____
The foregoing instrument was subscribed and sworn
before me this _____day of _____, 20____, by
_____ (name of affiant).


 Seal _____
```

Notary's Signature _____
Registration No. _____
Commission Expiration Date:_____

Copy Certification

Commonwealth of_____
City/County of _____
I certify this to be a complete, full, true and exact
reproduction of the original document.
Certified this _____ day of _____, 20_____.

Seal

                  Notary's Signature_____
                  Registration No._____
                  Commission Expiration Date:_____

....

Certificate of Authority for an Electronic Notarial Act

I, _____ (name and title), certify that
_____ (name of electronic notary), the person
named as Electronic Notary Public in the attached or
associated electronic document, was commissioned as an
Electronic Notary Public for the Commonwealth of
Virginia and authorized to act as such at the time of
the document's electronic notarization. To verify this
Certificate of Authority for an Electronic Notarial
Act, I have included herewith my electronic signature
this ____ day of _____, 20____.

                          _____
                          Electronic signature and
                      Seal of commissioning official

  Notary's Registration Number:_____

DEPOSITION

The certificate for a transcribed deposition should comply with the following format:

State of_____   )
)SS:
County of _____)

Certificate of Officer Before Whom Deposition is Taken

I,_____(Name of Officer),
a_____(Title) do hereby certify that,
pursuant to_____(Specify the stipulation, notice or order of court under which the
deposition was taken) the deposition of _____(Name of Witness) was duly taken
at_____(Place) on_____(Date) at
_____ o'clock ___m. before me.
The said_____(Name of witness) was first duly sworn (or affirmed) by me according
to law to tell the truth, the whole truth and nothing but the truth and thereupon did testify
as set forth in the above transcript of testimony. The testimony was taken down in my presence
stenographically by_____(Name of stenographer) under my direction.

I do further certify that the above deposition is full, complete and true record of all the
 testimony given by the said witness.

_____
Officer

Credible Witness Certificate

```
Commonwealth of _____
County of _____
On this _____day of _____ 20 _____, before me,
_____, a Notary Public , the undersigned officer,
personally appeared _____, known to me (or
satisfactorily proven) to be the person(s) whose
name(s) is/are subscribed to the within instrument and
acknowledged that he/she/they executed the same for the
purposes therein contained.
```

◇◇◇◇◇◇◇◇◇◇◇◇◇◇◇◇◇◇◇◇◇◇◇◇◇◇◇◇◇◇◇◇◇◇◇◇

Always check your State or Commonwealth's Handbook and laws to make sure your seal and certificates comply with your State or Commonwealth laws.

◇◇◇◇◇◇◇◇◇◇◇◇◇◇◇◇◇◇◇◇◇◇◇◇◇◇◇◇◇◇◇◇◇◇◇◇

Self-Evaluation

Main role of a Notary Public:

_____
_____
_____
_____

Five common types of Notarial Acts

_____
_____
_____
_____

First step in a Notarial Act:

_____
_____
_____

Recommended steps during a Notarial Act:

_____

_____

_____

_____

_____

Acknowledgement:

_____

_____

_____

_____

_____

Jurat:

_____

_____

_____

_____

Difference between an Oath and an Affirmation:

_____
_____
_____
_____
_____

Copy Certification:

_____
_____
_____
_____
_____

Signature Witnessing:

_____
_____
_____
_____
_____

Signature by Mark:

_____
_____
_____
_____
_____

Traditional Notary:

_____
_____
_____
_____
_____

Electronic Notary (eNotary):

_____
_____
_____
_____
_____

WebCam Notary (Remote Notary):

_____

_____

_____

_____

_____

What Non-Lawyers Notaries CANNOT do:

_____

_____

_____

_____

_____

Notary Seal:

_____

_____

_____

_____

_____

Impartial Witness:

_____
_____
_____
_____
_____

Affidavit:

_____
_____
_____
_____
_____

Errors and Omission Insurance:

_____
_____
_____
_____
_____

Subscribing Witness:

_____
_____
_____
_____

Embosser:

_____
_____
_____
_____

Notary Signing Agent:

_____
_____
_____
_____

Notary Organizations:

_____

_____

_____

_____

_____

Name of this book:

_____

_____

_____

_____

_____

Name of Author:

_____

_____

_____

_____

_____

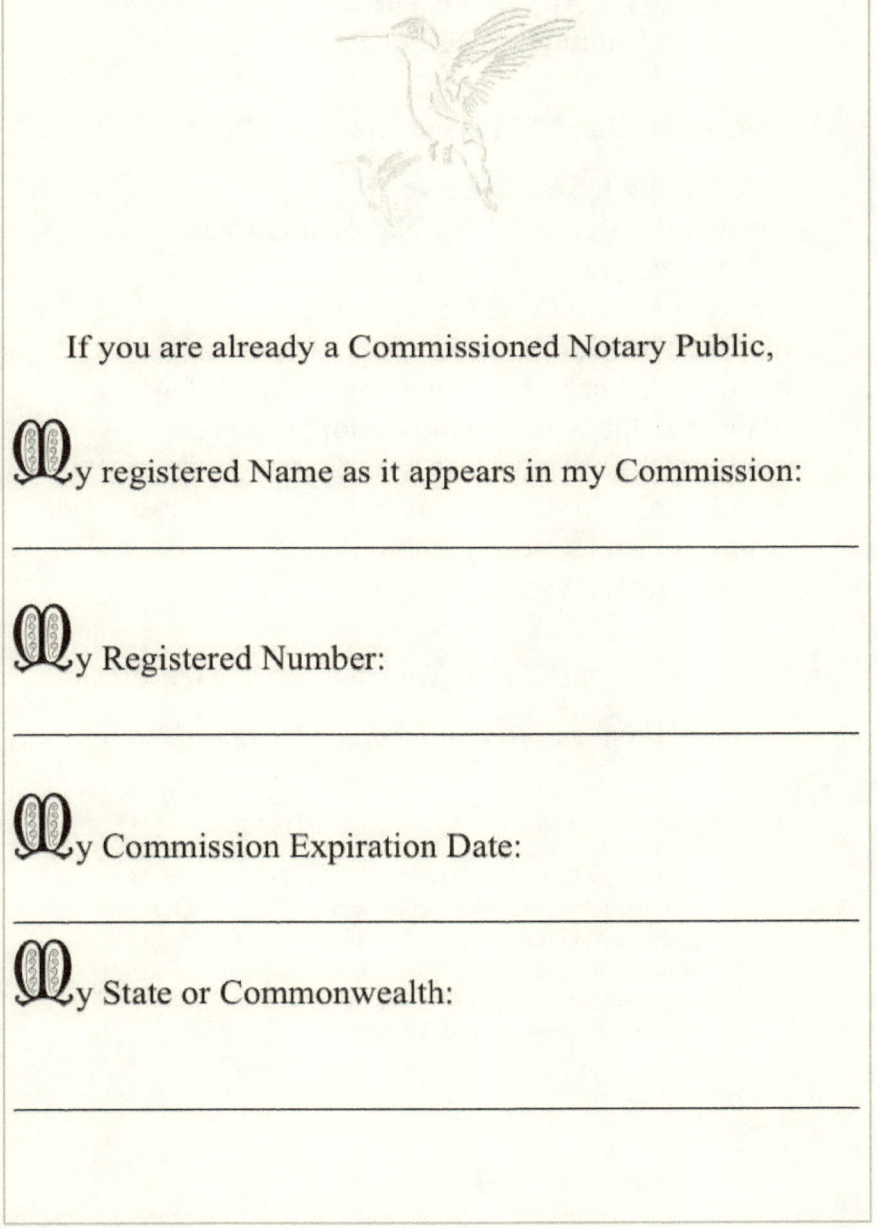

If you are already a Commissioned Notary Public,

$\mathfrak{M}$y registered Name as it appears in my Commission:

_____

$\mathfrak{M}$y Registered Number:

_____

$\mathfrak{M}$y Commission Expiration Date:

_____

$\mathfrak{M}$y State or Commonwealth:

_____

About the Author
Jeannie Eunice Franks-Belgrave

Born at Lackland AFB, San Antonio, TX.

Airman in the USAF Reserve.
Served in the Kentucky Air National Guard.
Air Force Veteran.
Alumni of Miami Dade College-AA.
Alma Matter: Florida International University-BFA.
Alumni of Asbury Theological Seminary-MDiv.
Ordained in the Non-Denominational Church.
Founder of KJViZion Ministries Corp.
Defender of the 1st Amendment of the US Constitution.
Commissioned as Notary Public.
Certified Notary Signing Agent.

Books: *Love and Truth, Notary Public Essentials,*

eNotary and Remote Notary Essentials.

Awards: Air Force Longevity Service Award, USAF.

Outstanding Unit Award (with 1 Oak Leaf Cluster) USAF.
Air Force Reserve Meritorious Service Medal (with 1 Oak Leaf Cluster) USAF.
Air Force Achievement Medal, USAF.
National Defense Service Medal, USAF. Global War on
Global War on Terrorism Medal, USAF.
Air Force Training Ribbon, USAF.

Perseverance Award, Detachment 155, AFROTC.

ow to Contact the Author

Subscribe to my Newsletter:
https://www.virginianotary.club/

Join me and be part of a great Network:

https://www.facebook.com/MyVirginiaNotary/

https://www.linkedin.com/in/jeannie-franks-490453167

References

Jeannie Franks' Notary notes.

5 Steps to a Flawless Notarization, page 5, Eight Edition. National Notary Association (NNA). 2017.

http://members.usnotaries.net/files/Virginia_Notarial_Certificates.pdf

https://en.wikipedia.org/wiki/Notary_public

https://www.google.com/search?
ei=DdA7W_HlJI_w_wSs3oGIDQ&q=notary+public+defined&oq=notary+public+defined&gs_l=psy-ab.
3..0j0i22i30k1l9.12927.14533.0.14645.8.8.0.0.0.0.164.879.0j6.6.0....0...1c.
1.64.psy-ab..2.6.878...0i67k1.0.cKCbuu1j2ZI

https://www.britannica.com/topic/notary

Experience.

Last minute tips:

When you sea the word "Seal" next to the signer's line for signature, it means it is the signer's signature that goes in that line.

Most likely, the notary's wording for notarization and seal is placed below or after the content of the document.

If you are like me and identify with the round stamp better than the rectangular one, here is a tip I learned from my latest Notary Teacher: "get the rectangular as well because some documents will only have space for a rectangular notary stamp."

I did not hesitate and ordered my rectangular stamp right away. When it arrived, it also had the state emblem which I thought it was cool.

In regard to the embosser. Even if your state or commonwealth does not require one, have one. Many clients feel their documents are properly notarized when they see the embosser's seal stamped in their documents. Also, when you implement the use of the golden or silver self-adhesive notarial seals along with the embosser, it gives your notarial act a nice touch. Remember, keep up high standards. As a Public Officer you are representing yourself and the State or Commonwealth that commissioned you.

Accessories Check List:

Designed for notaries who have difficulty reading small fonts or want to keep one entry per page.

Designed for notaries who want to keep 2 entries per page and also the number of the book, first entry, and last entry for better organization.

The Log Books above are available at
http://www.lulu.com/spotlight/NotaryPublic

Secured Carry-All Bag
for the Mobile Notary.

Blue and Black Pens.

Hand Sanitizer.

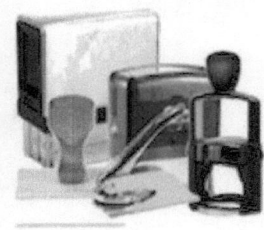

Seal and wording for certificates Stamps. Embosser (if needed). Keep them clean. Blue ink is my preferred ink.

Loose Certificates.

Calculator. Most notaries I know have a sharp mind. One never knows. Some clients like to see a calculator on the table.

Chargers for anything and everything electronic you use or have during your mobile notarial acts; mobile, computer, tablet, and other portable peripherals.

Water. The Notary wants to stay hydrated.

First Aid Kit for unexpected paper cuts, headaches, etc. Notary wants to keep a polite attitude at all times during notarial acts.

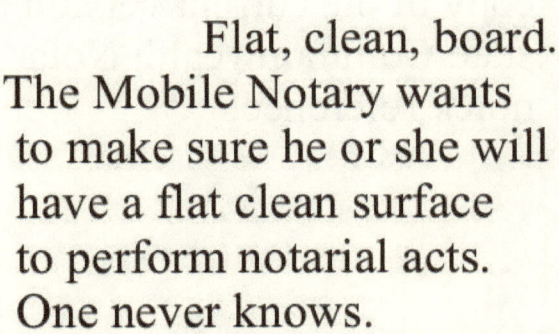

Flat, clean, board. The Mobile Notary wants to make sure he or she will have a flat clean surface to perform notarial acts. One never knows.

Printed version of the
current State/Commonwealth
Notary Handbook.

The Mobile Notary wants to keep a printed
copy of the current version of his or her
state/Commonwealth Notary Handbook for
quick reference.

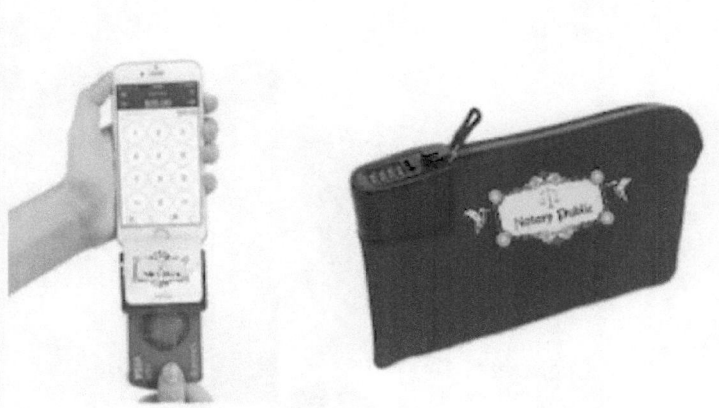

Unless the Mobile Notary Public will get paid direct deposit by another entity or is not going to charge a fee for notarial acts, it is advisable to carry a credit card reader and a secured cash bag.
There are credit card readers that are compatible with laptops.

Laptop with all the accessories it needs to function well and keep it clean.

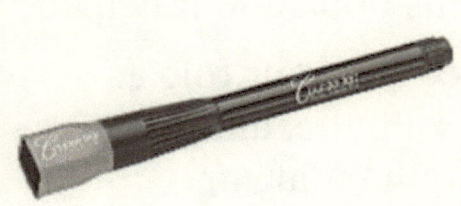

The following is said by the people who sell this pen: "Use the Counterfeit Detector Pen to check for authentic U.S. currency paper. Special patented formula makes a light mark on good bills or a dark mark on suspect bills. Also authenticates driver's licenses, passports, foreign currencies and other secure documents."

Not a bad idea to have as an accessory. As you may be aware of, fraud is a reality. This is why Notaries Public play an important role each and every time they perform a notarial act.

$\mathfrak{H}$ope you enjoyed this book and it helped you somehow to reflect on your role as Public Officer, Notary Public, and you as a positive contributor to the State or Commonwealth that commissioned you.

$\mathfrak{N}$ow, go have some fun making sure that people are who they say they are when requesting your notarial services and making sure that your part as Notary Public is performed with excellency.

Thank you Seasoned Notaries Public for keeping our country standing up and societies moving forward with your notarial contribution.

Some of you are having the privilege to witness the transitions on how Notarial Acts are performed, from ink to paper to Apps configurations.

Thank You

Practice

Place your stamps straight
and between the lines.

_____

_____

_____

_____

_____

_____

Your Notes:

82

Notary Public Essentials

Special note to the brand new Commissioned Notary Public:

First, congratulations! Your position as public officer goes beyond what one imagines when first becoming an official Notary Public. Remember, always check the laws of the State or Commonwealth that granted you the commission. On that note, read over and over what type of Identifications are allowed during a notarial act. Make sure the Identification is current and has all the elements required by the laws of your State or Commonwealth. Also, there are many types of identification, from military IDs to foreign IDs. It is highly recommended to get the current ID guides. There are two books titled: "I.D. Checking Guide"; one is the USA/Canada Edition, and the other one is the International edition. Get both if possible or when possible to you. Also, invest on a dual pen specially designed to detect counterfeit money and IDs. Use it during notarial acts. Read well about what type of IDs are acceptable and if a thumbprint is required in your State or Commonwealth at the time of recording notarial acts on the Notary's LogBook.

All the best to you in your journey as Notary Public. I hope you drop a line or two on my Facebook Page
https://www.facebook.com/MyVirginiaNotary.

Jeannie E. Franks

Notary Public Essentials

Notary Public Essentials

Notary Public Essentials

Notary Public Essentials

Notary Public Essentials

Notary Public Essentials

Notary Public Essentials

Notary Public Essentials

www.ingramcontent.com/pod-product-compliance
Lightning Source LLC
Chambersburg PA
CBHW022108170526
45157CB00004B/1531